MEET ME HERE AT DAWN

sophie klahr

MEET ME HERE AT DAWN

MEET ME HERE AT DAWN
© 2016 BY SOPHIE KLAHR

COVER & INTERIOR DESIGN: ALBAN FISCHER

FIRST EDITION, 2016
ISBN 978-1-936919-42-0

PRINTED IN THE UNITED STATES OF AMERICA

PUBLISHED BY YESYES BOOKS
1614 NE ALBERTA ST
PORTLAND, OR 97211
YESYESBOOKS.COM

KMA SULLIVAN, PUBLISHER
STEVIE EDWARDS, SENIOR EDITOR, BOOK DEVELOPMENT
JILL KOLONGOWSKI, MANAGING EDITOR
MARK DERKS, FICTION EDITOR, *VINYL*
ALBAN FISCHER, GRAPHIC DESIGNER
BEYZA OZER, DEPUTY DIRECTOR OF SOCIAL MEDIA
AMBER RAMBHAROSE, CREATIVE DIRECTOR OF SOCIAL MEDIA
PHILLIP B. WILLIAMS, COEDITOR IN CHIEF, *VINYL*
JOANN BALINGIT, ASSISTANT EDITOR
MARY CATHERINE CURLEY, ASSISTANT EDITOR
JOHNNA C. GURGEL, ASSISTANT EDITOR, PUBLICITY
COLE HILDEBRAND, ASSISTANT EDITOR
CARLY SCHWEPPE, ASSISTANT EDITOR, *VINYL*
HARI ZIYAD, ASSISTANT EDITOR, *VINYL*

CONTENTS

MEET ME HERE AT DAWN

PRAYER

In your voice, the word *Body* is a well
and *Mouth*

                the pail dipping
into long hours I am without you

VETIVER

As if that name could guide my restlessness,
some knowledge of the soil it grows in best:
the type of roots contained inside the soap
inside our first hotel room, creek-scent swelled
so, pressed against the ocean's salt which rocks
all night against the steep dune's edge, this scent
high field after rain, an old skin leaned in-
to. A candle lit. The dead are washed in
the way I'll wash my body now, so care-
   ful to be clean in case God comes and wants
to touch my mouths, wants to hide pieces of
my self in me. Now when you feel your self
unraveled, you fly back to my body
with your piece of God. Now whose hand is whose?

SAY WHEN

if you are a man made of birds
if you are a bureau

if chest, if cage

if you are a weather
worn out, say when

if the space between us makes
a dog named vacancy

if I contain all possible crimes

if I can return to the night
in the field, to lift from the grass
the shape of your wife

I can wait and not wait, want
and be a seed, a vessel, believe

the bedroom's red light catching
sweat like cinders in your hair

if I pay close attention, if I stay very still
if I notice how stupid we are

if, say, I was always on fire

ONE SLAUGHTER

What aperture makes a woman?
I bring the sea in. I do no research
whatsoever.

Pollen sighs shawl-like citywide,
yellow with futures, then overnight
in the cold snap
all the bees go down.

       I crouch to watch—
one creeps along the street. I note
who turns to judge my grief.

In this hotel, rooms are shaped like cabins of a ship, the wallpaper velvet like moss. Late daylight splits over the river into the room into the skin our bodies make—

                            this room on the river a light you can taste.
Last week you lost your wedding ring at the shore, you've yet to replace it and I daydream you won't, but no one can really live two lives.   Instead, one learns to move differently, to make air thread between each piece that is torn—   how, if you break a bone, you can stave off the pain by breathing into it

BEGINNERS

this is the living room. this is the moon. this is us kissing; that's us in the mirror. *that over there?* is new jersey. these are the cherries you bought on 14th street. this is you holding the pits in your palm. this is my spit. this wild, this wilderness. this is the hole in the story.

hello to you, keel.   hello to you, field.   these are the flags in the wind on the pier. this is the pattern,   the sun on our skin

      this rattle, this frame   this busy the mind

us at the movies: that's us in the film.   this is exhaustion, this is the hudson; so many rollerblades, so many tiny dogs, and how many people there are in new york. this is your thumb in the roof of my mouth. this is okay. this is enough.

MIMESIS PRAXEOS

In my dream last night a voice behind us said, *Take One*.

We speak of the absence of guilt like a mantra,
preserving a semblance

of order. Your wedding ring hums
from the kitchen table like static.

An extra asks if the movie we're making is cathartic.
        Cathartic? you mutter, *cathartic?*

Endlessly, we discuss fidelity, what to keep visible.
How to describe the house without burning it down.

TRICK

Houdini would hide copies of the same key all over his body
during any trick with a lock. You give me a key
to one of your houses; How do we get out of this one?
I should be more careful and copy your way of touching
just about everyone to make everyone feel
a little special.
I should learn to be your type of thief.
Tell me more about Houdini—
I know he was your hero as a child,
when sometimes   (*Presto!*)
your father appeared like a rabbit,
hurtling out of the night—

TO CRADLE

I like knowing there was never a time you would've been
unable—too small or too young—to hold me.

Someone might have helped, said *Careful with the baby or*
Put your hand under her neck, like this, and shown you.

Touch me like that when you come back—

think of how you became a compass
in the moment you first held your child.

I study you
like the first river I saw,

how I learned to get home
by following the river, learned

how everything goes downstream
at some point, disappears

in mornings before we speak

and all is cradle, then current,
current, then cradle.

SUCH UNFORTUNATES

It doesn't get better, it gets different. Ask God,
Clean House, Help Others. Try taking a trip, not taking a trip,
swearing off forever, with and without solemn oath. This too
shall pass: this rented office space, these folding chairs,

this night where women droop into the room like low fog,
bused in from a halfway house for those with infants.
Each holds a tiny body over her world and I wonder
which of us will die first. Their eyes wash over me.

After the meeting, I am murmuring sobriety's aphorisms

    (How does it go? Is it   *Ask God,* or *Trust*—)

until something pulls taut between us, splits— you say,
I want you to beg for it on all fours,   and I say, *I am.*

OPENING NIGHT

Dear Dog, touch each photograph,
each texted frame of my spit-

wet skin suggesting a scene
    to be lit and played

Translate my body like Adam naming animals

I've been trying not to mention your marriage but
but they say a gun onstage   must go off, so
    let's get to it:

Here is a photograph where my legs appear to you
as wings   Here is a photograph of my eye you call

a bright pill   Here, there are no photographs
of my hands   Here, systems of lips

            Here, (turn the body)

the spinal column, then buried:
clustered nerve-stars

    galloping from palm to cunt to sole, this picture

where the bed is a feeling you can't shake, a migraine,   a cage
containing sea stones,

a script, a string of red lights—
It's a dream:

there's a girl, a bed, a gun, a fire
You want her to be a body of water   a city   you can disappear

    into for awhile   The gun goes off and something
like a shard of glass slips, to nestle

at the edge of your eye, forever…

You want to click your heels together three times but
    that's the wrong movie—*And you were there, and you, and you—*

    You lean over your mother, to kiss her goodbye—
A woman on the street yells *Get out of the movie*

There's a bed, a fire, a girl, a gun

When we speak from afar
you always say

you're going home

THE FLOODED FIELD

Imagine an orange, cut into slices, on a plate on a bed
on a night in April, under the slow clicking fan.
I have memorized the sound of your tongue's slight
push on the roof of your mouth, as when you say *Body*.

Softly, say *Body*.
Imagine a field flowering, an updraft
of sulfur, a bird fading
somewhere nearby. Imagine

almost nothing for miles.
Let's bring a dog from the left, gold
streaming across the wet field like a paper fortune
slipped from your palm into the wind and gone.

I am carefully drawing a river, then a boat
at the edge of the scene. The boat
its own cool light we swim toward
to examine the tether.

50 WAYS

i can turn the space of him over in my hands

see if it comes apart
if it's permeable

does it stand on its own
keep time

could it clothe me?
could I swallow it?

will it stick

in the bloodstream
will it thin?

today you said you will call at noon at one and you are in a different time zone maybe
you think I am also but now

it is after one everywhere.
let's try this again:

if morality has a fiber to it can it heal itself?

once you puncture convention can you put the air back in?

will it float   will it rot?
can you translate the gesture?

are there truly
fifty ways to leave

could you try on a way?

set up a little chair there
a little desk

draw a window
draw a door

pretend it is a space you could live in, his absence.

Here is the story of Do Not Disturb signs, the slippage of hotel stationaries
pocket mints   lotions   matchbooks

the tarot card you gave me of a woman bound in chains or does she hold the chains.
The paper bag of cash brought to avoid a paper trail. *Hush money*, we laugh. Sort-of laugh.

You slip the cash into my shoes, slip out to the hall to call your wife
and I watch the river / highway / skyline / hills

We must be somewhere, right?

There are words I still always misspell   *Silhouette, Judgment*   still
        I confuse Lay and Lie

            Hush Chicago   Hush New York   Hush Orlando   Hush Miami

Here is my handwriting you mistook once for yours.
Here is the footnote containing other women, other flights.

DEPARTURES

Go on and make a bed in the grass
Go on and cup the face of the deer in your hands

Go on

Too much is sacred; I sing a small night song in the refrigerator's glow, I pray
    for the angels to stop coming but I know they will always come and pray instead
    for a very good place to hide, for a magic trick I can do with scarves
                  and a nickel

Go and bleed somewhere else not on the couch for god's sake

~~

A red plastic bird, its paint worn away,
whistled from the chain

of our kitchen's chandelier
    and only my father could reach it.

Wire feet he wound onto the links.

Something special about the bird—
                its cause and effect,

                the way he made it call

~~

Go away, this is my space behind the winter coats

Go away, this is my cardboard box

you cannot come inside

~~

Christmas, black ice in the headlines;

Dusk, and the small bulbs blink on in the trees

Dusk, and the bar's neon gives
a little sigh—

windows lit, the streets wet, the looking in while jingling a little change in your pocket
then turning away

DIAGNOSIS

so his life snapped back, a bough
pulled down then released
      into the dusk,

unearthing a sound in the air
that had always been

inaudibly in motion—

I turn towards the sound.
         watch it drifting

in my brother

like a red silk in water

AFTER THE WAR I DREAMT OF NOTHING BUT THE WAR

When the nurse on the phone won't tell me
where you are, I turn my body into wind

    troubling the city of hospitals.
Slang of nurses, blood numbers, legalities;

my disease has made me fluent in Emergency;

at the front desks they are not allowed
to say you are here, but they do not say

you are not here, they say *If he was here*
would you want to send back a note?

        and I write three notes
in three hospitals, watching the nurse

for her smooth head's small twitch that says,
        He isn't here.

It's Mercy Hospital, finally, that has you.
And again, because you are not family

I am a waiting room, crowded with sound.

Something-something-terror
jangles across the television: old news.

Two children, strangers, discuss superhero du jour:

Iron Man.   Iron Man can   he can fly, he has guns, he can turn
into whatever he needs.

The crows have come back
to the city for the spring. They swerve

over each river, crying to one another

Come here come here come here come here
come here. Come here come here

TWELVE YEARS LATER

I can imagine the baby pooling away from me

like smoke, imagine doctors soft as doves

beating their wings, murmuring, guiding the dark plume

into a bucket. Into a bag. Then afterwards, smoothing

a sheet over me. No, a veil. If there's such thing as a soul,

two flickered in me for years. Then one.

SUMMER JOB, JUNE

There are cream sounds at dusk, and garden stones
brought from the lake. Lace curtains, dim gold vines
along bedroom walls. Low moon—lavender,
ravens; the scent of algae in the air;
damp chalk children left on the street last night;
flies shimmering over a small dead bird.
One summer, a boy slipped, lost to the gorge
where he had been climbing with his brother.
When my brother visits, he slips nightly
into churches to touch their organs, &
I trail him, waiting outside the windows.
If he sees me, he will not play at all.
The boy who did not fall works the grounds here
    as a gardener. I often see him
kneeling, his hands slowly turning the earth.

THE LONG TAKE

Shy of Route 12, I cut along the lake
and step through the fence of dumpsters

behind the Lighthouse Grocery.
All the butcher boys have eyes like movie stars,

languid heart-throbs in their white coats
among the carcasses. We underestimate

what animal traffics are still within us,
the moral compass like a possum:

bewildered, nearly blind, a body of dust
climbing the dark.

In the fields are the Amish picking strawberries.
In the fields are the bones of a dog, blanched white by the sun.

HUMANITY

My mother opens the newspaper to a story in India where a man is attacked by a tiger at the edge of a city.   *Poor tiger* I say & my mother says   *What's wrong with you*

AT THE ROUND HOUSE

A childhood of lush wasp-haunted pears and dust
the thin light caught on the long-dead rat in the basement.

My brother and I were taken from the city
to someone's country home and allowed

wandering. A rock lifted: salamanders, black and specked
red, swam downstream; after the hill, inside the farmhouse

and old smell of horses, a cat at the edge of things.
If one thing could be restored to each of us, I'd ask for the sense

we had of ourselves when young, before I was afraid for him—
green and sneaky tumbling beings,

hissing together back at the big barn geese, close enough to see
the sinew of their necks, the tiny-razor teeth on their tongues,

before we'd turn
and run

AGAINST DESIRE

I dream there is a minnow in my body.
I dream its jaw unhinges on my eggs
and swallows every ghost.
I wake just as the meds are wearing off.
My anxious dreaming, Doctor? A nightmare?
I wouldn't call it that. I wouldn't call.
The morning rolls sideways, stumbles, re-sets.
Some teenage girl is crying on the train:

    But that was what you wanted, wasn't it?
Wasn't it?

SOME NOTES ON SHADOWS

I wept making love to a man old enough
to be my father. When we curved
into sleep, one of us contained
more shadow than the other.

      * *

A child's unfixed eyes swim
after complicated light on the wall.
It is sunset, a white hydrangea tree
at the window in the breeze.

      * *

Before your child can speak
she is scarcely a girl, but a thing you know
you could kill someone to save.
It is a rush of knowing—this shadow.

      * *

The story goes: my father first held me
one morning at the window of the hospital.
That is a mailbox, he told me,
that is a tree. He did not mention the shadow.

TWO STONES / SWALLOW

when is a woman like a well?   when she waits. stone pale, pistil,
a hush;   at the well's edge, a snake—
what else lives in a wall?   snake a scale of yet.   I drop a stone
into my mouth watch for the echo pass through my body.
does the well have an ebb, ever feel full?   not everything makes
a sound but how long to wait

////

when is a man like a throat?   when
            he is silent;
doing briefly what smoke does there.

black passage; peace hollow as a stem.
   in mania, the edges of everything have an out-

line only the sick can see. I mean, I saw.
what seeing did— that brutal.

sometimes, even speaking of it is a sickness.

ARRIVALS

After sex sometimes, there is blood on the sheets

                                        bright ciphers

The hush of the plane. How slow it feels

                                        this coming-to-earth

                    These masks falling from above not meant to save us

~~

Your beauty no shelter
Your word no shelter

To consider: I loved a hive of light
To consider: I came when he bit my palm

~~

For awhile, we denied everything our therapists said—it was a good way
of being together.

A hand on mine in the dark in the dark in the dark

~~

In the airport, trembling back to wonder if the oven is on.
How a hand curls a little in sleep;

the instinct to cup a hand around any flame

SLANT

which codes the luminous tree at your gate
which broad night renders its own wild leap

and to name the record of that as MEMOIR, i.e.
exemption from certainty,

spilt onto the belly
whose girth is a path through the dunes

this is allowed as is, as is
    losing the name of the organ you lost to necessity

the small pinging sadness of that:
you, veiled so deeply in each poem

that for a moment, I forget the truth of your body

————

the blast radius
the dearth of guilt

the cipher that shifts
from line to line

after a threat, a wait; leaving

separately from any crowd who knows us;

morality a thing to be caught
and no man born with it

————

MEMOIR:
form of doubles, of squinting, of lifting the dress;

the skittering of years

                    one woman melted
                    down from two

                    or three

repeat: your crooked teeth / a pattern of birds
as doubt, the chatter under our time

the steady mistake of strangers
believing me your wife

————

as I remember it / all this is true

DO YOU?

You asked once if I thought you shouldn't be married.   Perhaps (I think I said)
you married the wrong person. To each their poison, their chain, their joy. Their hospital,
their someone at home. Dependent, partner,   passenger, hostage.   To each their ring
and albatross. To each   their cross,   their pause.   To each their myth and law, their allergy
and pleasure. Each   to their frame, each to their mold. To each their fuel and code.
To marrying up, marrying in, marrying late. For the children. For the hell of it.

BEFORE RESULTS

What could we do with our sickness,
would we skin or husk or hurry it?
Worry under it? Carry it gently
as it will shatter if held
wrong—could we dull it, drown it?
Would our sickness itch also
above the waist, above the throat
and do we now doubt our odd fidelity?
Could we say for certain the other
was never sick before, never, with
another lover, studied their length
and asked, *What's this?* And now
what of our mouths? Would you kiss me?
Could we screw our sickness more deeply
inside of our skin? Could we manage to keep
our hands to ourselves until we healed and
will we? Will we heal? There's a light
that pours from us— is it light? Can we
carve it from our bodies, burn it, offer it up?

DELETED SCENE 1 (METHOD ACTING)

dumb tangle, gristle.   (take eight)

our odor all flinch and chase,

the camera a sound over us. in this scene

one of us is chained, a dog. the other,

a child, pushing food with a stick towards the dog.

we stand in our hunger like a room, forgetting our lines.

it has a purity; each of us believes we are the dog.

when I rehearse well, the words sink in,

    the character now whole

within me and ungovernable.

"I ONCE SAW A PIMP WHO HAD A HARD-ON WHILE WRITING TO HIS GIRL, PLACE HIS HEAVY COCK ON THE PAPER AND TRACE ITS CONTOURS"

I still have somewhere the outline
you traced of your cock. It was the exact size
of my throat, some fraction of the plank
I pushed aside when young,
to slip into the neighbor's yard, another
kind of paradise. I knew it
as I know my mouth,
crossed into the room of knowing it,
drawn in by a line you read aloud
concerning a field and what happened
in the field. Beyond the fence was
a tongue of uncut grass I could lie in,
my body's first breaking and entering.
I told my hands, *Go*, muscles,
Go, and pushed aside the plank
where it hung by a single nail
and opened my mouth
to all the trouble to come.

LESSON

Something about the quality of her tears, you said,
to explain how you knew

the friend who wept in your arms
knew her husband to be having an affair.

In class, I draw a man dragging another man
on a leash. I say the background

in this photograph is blurred—
    the light is dim   nothing's recognizable.

I ask my students what they feel, seeing this,
and they search my face for the right answer.

Multiple choice: Pity?
Guilt? Nothing?

I let the camera zoom out, draw,
around the men, a stage—

lavish curtains framing
the scene, an audience in silhouette.

I ask, *Is this different?*

Try to imagine, you said,
how I felt. You said,

That's how the corpse of the deer is
consumed by maggots:

first the asshole, tongued
by dozens of tiny mouths.

IT WAS THE NIGHTINGALE AND NOT THE LARK

His absence makes me out of mind. Out, heart—fucked limb.
There's no hole I haven't licked

or liked or longed for of his. *Unplug*, he says, meaning our affair
and what it should do, how the thread

should shudder out. I shrug. Absence: the fondness,
the foundering. Fickle choke. Pilot light.

your ring striking my ringlessness   rattling in another lobby, alert beside our luggage—
   adolescent, swollen, O

I've come to believe morality exists

   with a great intrinsic cavity:
      first temple, engine of faith, doubt field—

      it is the fifth year of our affair.   what have we brought forth?

it's fall, and we are staying in a small town by a river   we are saying
     divorce aloud, saying   *child*

the interior of the elevator is made entirely of mirrors, and makes our mouths move
   into the furthest possible distance

CELL PHOTO

text   : a bride wading into a pool (white bodice
                laces trail the surface)

text   : the desert outside your motel room

text   : the pool beneath the window

text   :

text   : thorns that found your arm
                pronouncing your blood in two lines

here
here

there is no glossary not for this

no one teaches us to breathe deeply
        then one day there is a doctor and you are half-dressed

breathe deeply he says,
and touches a cold metal spot to your back

is this all breathing is?

now cough he says

is this all?

just thorns doing, you said, *what thorns do*

MERCY

Walking onto the shore without a plan,
without my other mouth.

The guttural of Us:
full, a warm black sound,
born, knit—

    How to leave?   Thus shocked
to blossom, thus accustomed, heat-sure
and solid?

The risk grows abstract—

What offering's expanded?
       We're past departures;
How to split again?

We eat and eat and eat
and still our hands are clean.

GRACE

Night comes down
through the trees, cups my face
   upwards—*Here, Sweetie,*
the way you'd say it.

I find Orion's belt—three knots
bright at his hips.

The wild brush around me
keeps singing, places a palm
over my eyes.

KAIROS

Where an edge should order, all is smear, blush:

same cordgrass, same song;
    flash of wing, longing

~~

Why are we said to *fall* in love, and not to be cast?
The world is without waiver; there is nowhere
else to go

~~

cast (v.):   to throw something onto the seashore
to make something (light or shadow)   appear in a place

to generate   a sense of uncertainty

to remove or banish something from your mind   decisively

and often with difficulty   to throw somebody or something somewhere,
                                                especially   in a brutal way

to select the players   to mold

to drop or lose something
to add or calculate something

to shed or leave something, for example, a skin

                              ~~

Here is another translation:

We sit watching fires the dusk
beach dwellers have set—

dusk at the same shore
where we first met:

I am only allowed beauty like this once, I'd thought.

Even at dusk,
something about the light

cast over the ocean is blinding,
a right-warm blinding, the very same way

we've always made each other happy.

The title of this collection came to me through Cass McCombs's song of the same title, and has been employed with his blessing. Many references and fragments herein come from Kenneth Patchen's *The Journal Of Albion Moonlight*, Simone Weil's *Gravity and Grace*, Shakespeare's *Romeo and Juliet*, and the *Big Book of Alcoholics Anonymous*. *BEGINNERS* was inspired by the 2012 movie of the same title, written and directed by Mike Mills. *SOME NOTES ON SHADOWS* was inspired by Gregory Orr's poem of the same title. *BEFORE RESULTS* is inspired by the poem "As From A Quiver Of Arrows" by Carl Phillips. *50 WAYS* contains thoughts from Anne Carson's "Cassandra Float-Can," and is named after Paul Simon's "50 Ways To Leave Your Lover." *SLANT* contains thoughts from John Patrick Shanley and James Anthony Froude. *"I ONCE SAW A PIMP WHO HAD A HARD-ON WHILE WRITING TO HIS GIRL, PLACE HIS HEAVY COCK ON THE PAPER AND TRACE ITS CONTOURS"* takes its title as a direct quote from Jean Genet's *Our Lady Of The Flowers*, encountered via Wayne Koestenbaum's essay "The Darling's Prick." *OPENING NIGHT* references an idea from Anton Chekov, nods to *The Wizard of Oz*, and is inspired in part by Albert Goldbarth's essay "The Space." *THE FLOODED FIELD* is partly in conversation with Robert Duncan's "Often I Am Permitted To Return To A Meadow." *AT THE ROUND HOUSE, DIAGNOSIS,* and *SUMMER JOB, JUNE* are for my younger brother Ben, with deep love and faith in his indomitable spirit. *AFTER THE WAR I DREAMT OF NOTHING BUT THE WAR* is for Ryan, and dedicated to all those on the Road of Happy Destiny.

ACKNOWLEDGMENTS

Many of these poems first appeared, sometimes in different versions, in the following publications, and the author is grateful to the readers and editors for their careful attention: *1110*, *American Poetry Review*, *Anti-*, *BOAAT*, *B O D Y*, *California Journal Of Poetics*, *Connotation Press*, *Interrupture*, *Linebreak*, *Ninth Letter*, *Oh No Magazine*, *[PANK]*, *Pebble Lake Review*, *Ploughshares*, *Public Pool*, *Revolver*, *The Rumpus*, *Southern Humanities Review*, *Sycamore Review*, *The Journal*, *The Offending Adam*, *Tupelo Quarterly*, *TYPO*, and *Washington Square Review*.

GRATITUDES

Gratitude for shelter, space, and support given during the gestation of this book:
Tin House Writer's Workshop, University of Houston, Atlantic Center for the Arts, Ed Dadey, and Cass McCombs; love to my ultra-patient and generous family of origin; love to my ultra-patient and inspiring family of choice; love to my poet-brother Matthew Siegel.

Gratitude for guidance:
D.A. Powell, Terrance Hayes, Kelle Groom, and Gregory Orr. Special gratitude to YesYes Books publisher KMA Sullivan, and deep gratitude to Jim Daniels, my first mentor.

DEDICATION

for Nick, with relief, on the other side

SOPHIE KLAHR's writing appears in publications such as *American Poetry Review* and *Ploughshares*. Her interdisciplinary work includes collaborations with the contemporary dance theatre collective inFluxdance and the artist Dorothy Hoover. Born in Pittsburgh, she lives mostly in Los Angeles. She is the author of *Meet Me Here At Dawn* (YesYes Books, 2016).

ALSO FROM YESYES BOOKS